EAU CLAIRE DISTRICT LIBRARY
6528 East Main Street
P.O. Box 328
EAU CLAIRE, MI 49111

W9-ALL-910

J
363.34
Wor

WORLD BOOK'S
LIBRARY OF NATURAL DISASTERS

VOLCANOES

WORLD
BOOK

a Scott Fetzer company
Chicago
www.worldbookonline.com

EAU CLAIRE DISTRICT LIBRARY

T 142370

World Book, Inc.
233 N. Michigan Avenue
Chicago, IL 60601
U.S.A.

For information about other World Book publications, visit our Web site at
http://www.worldbookonline.com or call **1-800-WORLDBK (967-5325).**

For information about sales to schools and libraries, call **1-800-975-3250 (United States);**
1-800-837-5365 (Canada).

2008 revised printing
© 2008 World Book, Inc. All rights reserved. This book may not be reproduced in whole or
in part in any form without prior written permission from the publisher.

WORLD BOOK and the GLOBE DEVICE are registered trademarks or trademarks of
World Book, Inc.

Library of Congress Cataloging-in-Publication Data

Volcanoes.
        p. cm. -- (World Book's library of natural disasters)
    Summary: "A discussion of major types of natural
disasters, including descriptions of some of the most
destructive; explanations of these phenomena, what
causes them, and where they occur; and information
about how to prepare for and survive these forces of
nature. Features include an activity, glossary, list of
resources, and index"--Provided by publisher.
    Includes bibliographical references and index.
    ISBN 978-0-7166-9815-9
    1. Volcanoes--Juvenile literature.
I. World Book, Inc.
QE521.3.V6425 2007
551.21--dc22
                                2007006669

World Book's Library of Natural Disasters
Set ISBN: 978-0-7166-9801-2

Printed in China
2 3 4 5 6 12 11 10 09 08

Editor in Chief: Paul A. Kobasa

Supplementary Publications
    Associate Director: Scott Thomas
    Managing Editor: Barbara A. Mayes

Editors: Jeff De La Rosa, Nicholas Kilzer,
    Christine Sullivan, Kristina A. Vaicikonis,
    Marty Zwikel

Researchers: Cheryl Graham, Jacqueline Jasek

Manager, Editorial Operations
    (Rights & Permissions): Loranne K. Shields

Graphics and Design
    Associate Director: Sandra M. Dyrlund
    Associate Manager, Design: Brenda B. Tropinski
    Associate Manager, Photography: Tom Evans
    Designer: Matt Carrington

Product development: Arcturus Publishing Limited
Writer: Chris Oxlade
Editors: Nicola Barber, Alex Woolf
Designer: Jane Hawkins
Illustrator: Stefan Chabluk

Acknowledgments:

Corbis 10, 15, 29 (Reuters), 12 (Jim Sugar), 13 (Robert Holmes), 16 (Gary Braasch), 18 (Imelda Medina/ epa),
    19, 20, 41 (Roger Ressmeyer), 21 (Earl & Nazima Kowall), 26, 37 (Corbis), 27 (Rykoff Collection),
    28 (Yann Arthus-Bertrand), 30, 31 (Jacques Langevin/ Corbis Sygma), 39, 42 (Bettmann),
    40 (Jeremy Bembaron/Corbis Sygma).

G. Brad Lewis: cover/ title page.

Science Photo Library 8 (Prof. Stewart Lowther), 9 (Alan Sirulnikoff), 11, 22 (Bernhard Edmaier), 17 (Jack Fields),
    23, 24, 25 (Science Photo Library), 32 (Robert M Carey, NOAA), 33 (Gary Hincks), 38 (NASA).

Shutterstock 5 (Bychkov Kirill Alexandrovich), 35 (Todd Mestemacher).

TABLE OF CONTENTS

Glossary There is a glossary of terms on pages 45-46. Terms defined in the glossary are in type **that looks like this** on their first appearance on any spread (two facing pages).

Additional resources Books for further reading and recommended Web sites are listed on page 47. Because of the nature of the Internet, some Web site addresses may have changed since publication. The publisher has no responsibility for any such changes or for the content of cited sources.

WHAT IS A VOLCANO?

A volcano is an opening in Earth's **crust** through which ash, gases, and **molten** rock from below ground erupt onto Earth's surface or into the **atmosphere.** The word *volcano* is also used to describe the cone-shaped mountain or hill created by accumulated ash and rock at the site of the opening.

Parts of a volcano

A typical volcano has a **cone** made up of material from its past **eruptions.** Below the volcano is a **magma** *(MAG muh)* **chamber,** which contains molten rock. (Molten rock is called **magma** when it is below Earth's surface, and **lava** when it is above.) The magma rises through a central tube, called a **conduit,** to an opening on the surface, called a **vent.** Magma may also emerge from **side vents.** The typical bowl-shaped depression at the top of a volcano is called a **crater.**

Volcanic eruptions

Some volcanoes erupt only rarely, others occasionally, and some continually. Volcanoes erupt when magma collects in giant pockets deep under the ground. Pressure inside the pockets forces the magma through the rocks above, resulting in a volcanic eruption.

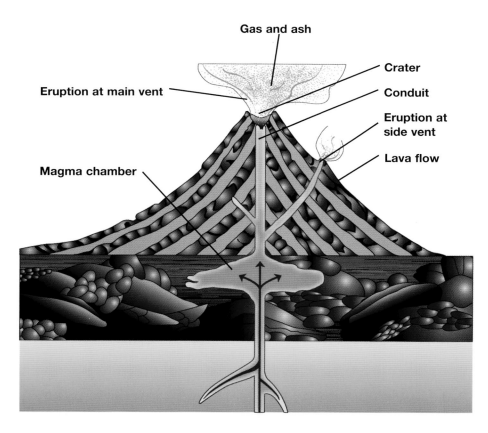

Gas and ash

Crater

Eruption at main vent

Conduit

Eruption at side vent

Lava flow

Magma chamber

Magma rises from deep underground through a conduit and other tubes to emerge from vents.

Volcanic hazards

Volcanic eruptions are one of nature's most dangerous events, and hundreds of thousands of people have died in them. Of the hazards created by a volcano, the lava flow itself is usually the least dangerous. In most instances, lava moves at about 6 miles (10 kilometers) per hour, so people and animals can usually escape from it. The flying rocks, called **pyroclastic** *(py ruh KLAS tihk)* **bombs,** that are ejected from a volcano are only somewhat more hazardous than lava flows, because these bombs usually fall near the volcano's vent.

Far more dangerous are clouds of hot gases and ash called **pyroclastic flows.** Another term for these flows is *nuée ardente,* French for *glowing clouds.* Pyroclastic flows can choke or poison people with gases, bury them with **debris,** and burn them with temperatures of up to 1100 °F (600 °C). A typical pyroclastic flow might advance at speeds of 50-150 miles (80-240 kilometers) per hour. People and animals cannot outrun pyroclastic flows. The secondary effects of volcanoes, such as **lahars** *(LAH hahrz)* and **tsunamis** *(tsoo NAH meez)* have also killed many thousands of people.

A volcano ejects a tall cloud of gas and ash—known as an eruption column.

THE WORD VOLCANO

The word *volcano* comes from Vulcan, the Roman god of fire, who served as the blacksmith for the gods. The ancient Romans believed that Vulcan lived on the island of Vulcano, off the southwest coast of what is now Italy. There, Vulcan made weapons for the other gods. Eruptions from the volcano on the island were thought to be sparks from Vulcan's forge.

Earth consists of three main layers. The outer layer, called the **crust,** is made up of solid rock. The crust is between 5 and 25 miles (8 and 40 kilometers) thick. In general, the crust under continents is thicker than that under oceans. Beneath the crust is a thick layer of rock called the **mantle.** The mantle is about 1,800 miles (2,950 kilometers) thick. The upper portion of the mantle is solid. In the lower mantle, the rock is so hot that, though solid, it flows. At the center of Earth is the **core.** The core is about 2,200 miles (3,550 kilometers) thick.

The crust and upper portion of the mantle form the **lithosphere** *(LIHTH uh sfihr).* The lower region of the mantle is called the **asthenosphere** *(as THEHN uh sfihr).* The location of many of the world's volcanoes is closely related to the activity of the **tectonic** *(tehk TON ihk)* **plates** that make up the lithosphere.

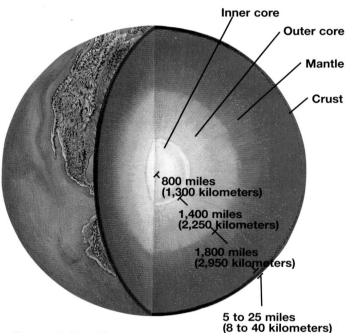

Inner core
Outer core
Mantle
Crust

800 miles
(1,300 kilometers)

1,400 miles
(2,250 kilometers)

1,800 miles
(2,950 kilometers)

5 to 25 miles
(8 to 40 kilometers)

Beneath Earth's solid crust are the mantle and the outer core and inner core.

Plates and boundaries

Earth's surface consists of about 30 tectonic plates. Some of these plates are small, but others are huge. These plates rest on top of the asthenosphere. The asthenosphere flows very slowly, so the tectonic plates above move slowly as well. A typical plate slides along at just 4 inches (10 centimeters) per year.

Most volcanoes occur at the plate boundaries, the regions where plates meet. At a **divergent plate boundary,** plates move away from each other. **Magma** rises up to fill the gap between the plates. Divergent plate boundaries are located mostly on ocean floors.

At a **convergent plate boundary,** plates move toward each other. One plate slides under the other and moves down into the asthenosphere. This process is called **subduction** *(suhb DUHK shuhn),* and the areas where it occurs are referred to as **subduction zones.** As the lower plate sinks, it carries water trapped within the rock deep into the hot mantle. The water eventually boils into the overlying mantle, causing it to melt. This produces pockets of magma that rise up through the upper plate to form volcanoes.

Hot spots

Some volcanoes are found at **hot spots**—places where an underground concentration of heat exists. This heat melts rock beneath the crust. The melted rock rises slowly to the surface, where it erupts as **lava.** Volcanoes caused by hot spots can occur far from plate boundaries, either on land or in the ocean. The volcanoes of the Hawaiian Islands in the Pacific Ocean are hot-spot volcanoes.

THE "RING OF FIRE"

There are subduction zones all around the edges of the Pacific Ocean, where the handful of plates that lie beneath the ocean are sinking beneath the surrounding plates. These subduction zones have created a horseshoe-shaped belt of volcanoes that stretches from New Zealand northwest to Indonesia and the Philippines, northeast to Japan, east to Alaska, and then along the west coast of the Americas to the southern tip of Chile. This belt of volcanoes is known as the "Ring of Fire."

Volcanoes are often found near the boundaries between Earth's tectonic plates.

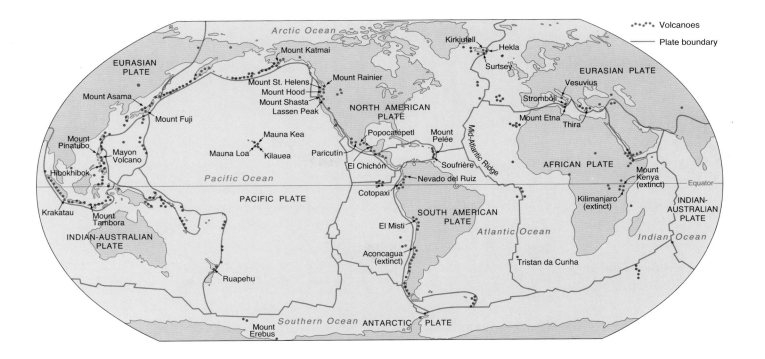

MOUNT SAINT HELENS

Mount Saint Helens is a volcano in the Cascade Mountains in the U.S. state of Washington. All the volcanoes in this area are caused by the **subduction** of the Pacific **tectonic plate** under the North American Plate. In 1980, Mount Saint Helens erupted explosively, killing 57 people.

The eruption

In the spring of 1980, small **earthquakes** were detected under Mount Saint Helens, and a bulge began to grow on the north side of the volcano as **magma** began to collect. By mid-May, the bulge had pushed upwards and outwards by about 450 feet (140 meters). On the morning of May 18, an earthquake triggered a **landslide** that caused the entire north side of the volcano's **cone** to collapse. This landslide was the largest in recorded history. More than 1,000 feet (300 meters) of the volcano's cone was destroyed, leaving a massive, horseshoe-shaped **crater.** A cloud of hot gas, ash, and rock exploded across the landscape. Instead of shooting upwards,

A pyroclastic flow rushing down the slopes of Mount Saint Helens after the initial eruption.

the initial blast erupted laterally, or out from the side of the volcano. An area of 250 square miles (650 square kilometers) was turned into an ash-covered wasteland with millions of trees flattened. The explosion also produced a column of ash 15 miles (24 kilometers) high.

The vast crater on Mount Saint Helens, seen from a ridge where trees were snapped off by the lateral blast of the initial eruption.

Warnings

The **volcanologists** *(vol kuh NOL uh jihstz)* who were monitoring Mount Saint Helens predicted the **eruption,** and local officials set up roadblocks around the danger area. Despite the warnings, some people wanted to see the eruption from a close vantage point. Charles McNerney and John Smart were about 6 miles (10 kilometers) away when the eruption occurred. They saw the mountainside collapse and a cloud racing toward them, which they later described as looking like an avalanche of black dust. They drove at speeds of up to 80 miles (130 kilometers) per hour to escape the cloud.

LUCKY ESCAPE

On the morning of May 18, a group of people were camping 14 miles (22 kilometers) north of the volcano, outside the region that had been cordoned off as the danger area. Two of them, Bruce Nelson and Sue Ruff, later described to reporters the darkness that fell as the cloud from the eruption arrived. As the blast reached them, Nelson and Ruff fell into a hole left by the root ball of a tree that had been knocked over. This saved them from the additional falling trees, but their hair was singed and their skin burned by the heat. Others in their party were not so lucky that day and did not survive.

STUDYING VOLCANOES

Volcanologists, who study both **active** and **dormant** volcanoes, try to understand how and why volcanoes erupt. This knowledge helps them to predict **eruptions.** Major active volcanoes have observatories on or near them to monitor volcanic activity.

Techniques and tools

Volcanologists use a range of techniques and tools to monitor volcanoes. One of the most important tools is **seismology,** which is the study of **earthquakes.** Small earthquakes coming from under a volcano show that rocks are breaking apart or that **magma** or gas is moving deep under Earth's surface. Instruments called **seismometers** detect earthquakes. A network of seismometers is used to work out exactly where an earthquake happened.

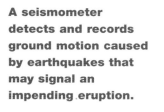

A seismometer detects and records ground motion caused by earthquakes that may signal an impending eruption.

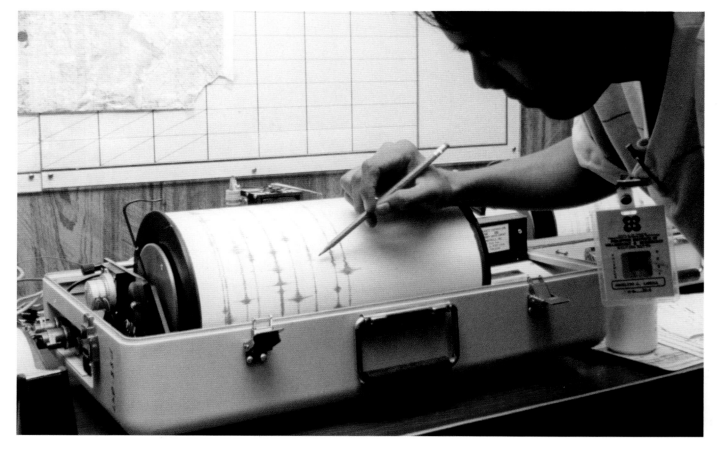

Because a volcano's top normally swells as magma pushes up from underneath, volcanologists monitor the **cone** for movement. Instruments called **tiltmeters** register both upward and downward movement. Volcanologists also use the **global positioning system** (GPS), a very accurate **satellite** navigation system. The GPS measures the exact position of markers placed in the ground and can show whether a volcano is swelling upward or outward.

The surface of a volcano warms up as magma comes close to the surface, so volcanologists monitor the ground temperature. They measure the temperature of gases coming from **vents.** They also collect samples of the deposits surrounding a volcano and of the gases being emitted. An increase in sulfur dioxide (SO_2) in these samples could show that magma is rising.

Volcanologists taking samples of deposits from the edge of a volcanic crater.

Remote sensing

Volcanologists use information collected by satellites to study volcanoes and eruptions. A satellite can measure the shape of a volcano using very accurate **radar** and can detect the surface temperature using cameras that are sensitive to heat. Cameras mounted on satellites can also photograph the spread of ash and gas from an eruption.

ERUPTION HISTORY

Many volcanoes erupt at regular intervals. The layers of ash and lava from previous eruptions can provide volcanologists with clues about what future eruptions might be like. They also indicate which areas are most likely to be at risk from **pyroclastic flows** and **lahars.** Nevertheless, volcanologists can always be surprised. Scientists observing Mount Saint Helens were not expecting the volcano to erupt in a lateral blast (see page 8).

MAGMA

Magma is the name for **molten** rock inside Earth. It normally forms under the **crust,** between 30 to 120 miles (50 to 200 kilometers) below the surface. Volcanoes occur where magma pushes its way through the rocks of the crust and emerges at the surface.

Magma types

Different chemical mixtures of the magmas cause differences in **viscosity.** Some magmas are quite fluid, having a consistency similar to cooking oil. Other magmas are thick and sticky, similar to molasses or tar. The chemical make-up of magma generally depends upon where the magma is formed. The magma that rises at **divergent plate boundaries** is normally thin and liquid. Magma that rises from **subduction zones** is normally thick.

Magma reaches the surface on the Hawaiian volcano Kilauea, and forms a lava flow.

Gas in magma

Magma also contains such gases as **water vapor,** carbon dioxide (CO_2), and sulfur dioxide (SO_2). When the magma is deep underground, the gases are dissolved in the magma. But as the magma nears the surface, the gases form bubbles. This is not unlike carbonated soft drinks. The pressure inside the bottle keeps the carbon dioxide gas dissolved in the drink mixture, but when the bottle is opened, gas bubbles rise to the top.

Eruptions of thin, liquid magma

The violence of an eruption depends on how liquid the magma is and the amount of gas it contains. Thin, liquid magma that contains only a little gas produces relatively gentle eruptions, because the magma pours easily from the ground. Liquid magma that contains a lot of gas produces **lava fountains** as the escaping gas flings lava into the air. Runny magma often pours down a volcano's slopes, creating lava flows. Eventually, the lava cools and turns solid.

Eruptions of thick magma

Thick magma with little gas produces steep **lava domes** because the lava does not flow easily and does not get far before it cools. Thick magma with lots of gas produces violent eruptions because the gas bubbles cannot move easily and, therefore, the bubbles blow the magma apart.

EAU CLAIRE DISTRICT LIBRARY

VOLCANIC NECKS

A **volcanic neck** (or volcanic plug) is a column made of solidified magma that once formed the core of a volcano. It is left standing after the softer rocks around it erode away. The Devil's Tower in Wyoming in the United States and Sugar Loaf Mountain in Rio de Janeiro, Brazil, are famous examples of volcanic necks.

The Devil's Tower in Wyoming is a column of solidified magma that was once the core of a volcano.

VOLCANIC HAZARDS

Volcanic eruptions create great hazards to people, buildings, roads and other structures, wildlife, forests, and crops. The direct hazards of a volcano include **lava flows** and **pyroclastic flows.** The least deadly of the direct hazards are slow-moving lava flows. However, lava flows have killed people, and they often destroy buildings and roads.

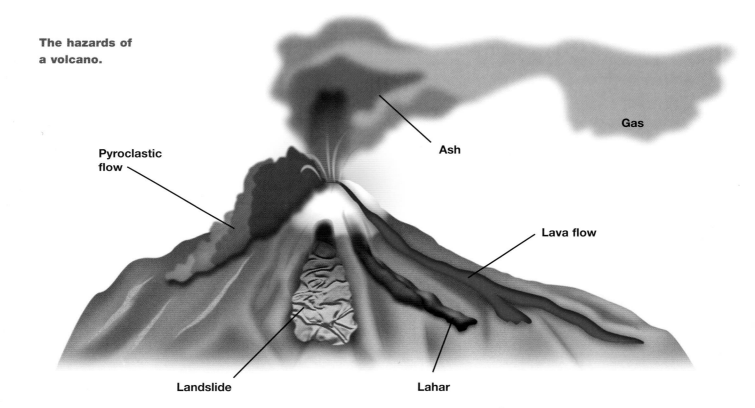

The hazards of a volcano.

Gas

Ash

Pyroclastic flow

Lava flow

Landslide

Lahar

The most deadly direct volcanic hazard is a pyroclastic flow, a cloud of hot gas and ash that travels mostly along the ground (see pages 22-23). Pyroclastic flows advance tens or hundreds of feet or meters per second, destroying everything in their path. Secondary hazards that result from volcanic eruptions include giant **landslides,** high-speed **lahars,** and **tsunamis** (see pages 28-29).

Explosive eruptions

Explosive volcanoes erupt rarely, but their eruptions are often quite violent. Such eruptions occur when thick, gas-filled **magma** moves to the surface. The gas in the magma starts to form bubbles, and eventually the pressure of the bubbles trying to expand causes the magma to explode. The explosion throws gas, ash, and pieces of rock high into the air, forming a tall cloud called an **eruption column.** These eruptions also cause pyroclastic flows and lahars. Successive eruptions can build up a steep-sided, cone-shaped volcano, made of layers of ash and **lava,** called a **stratovolcano.**

VOLCANIC EXPLOSIVITY

Volcanologists often rate the power of an eruption using the **Volcanic Explosivity Index** (VEI). Most eruptions have a VEI of 0 through 8, with 0 being not explosive at all and 8 ranking among the most explosive eruptions known. Mount Saint Helens had a VEI rating of 5. Each number represents around a 10-fold increase in power, so a VEI 5 eruption has 10 times the force of a VEI 4 eruption.

Active, dormant, and extinct

Volcanologists consider any volcano that has erupted in the last 10,000 years to be **active.** An active volcano that is not erupting or not about to erupt is classified as **dormant.** A volcano that is unlikely ever to erupt again is described as **extinct.**

A building is nearly engulfed by a lava flow on the slopes of Mount Etna, Italy.

PYROCLASTS

A field of pumice on the slopes of Mount Saint Helens in Washington state. Deposits like this are often left by pyroclastic flows.

Pyroclasts, also called pyroclastics, are fragments of **magma** ejected by a volcanic eruption. They are pushed upward by rapidly expanding gas bubbles. **Volcanologists** classify pyroclasts by their texture and size.

Volcanic ash

Volcanic ash is made up of tiny particles of solidified magma. Some particles are as small as grains of flour; others are as large as grains of sand. Ash is created when bubbly magma is blown apart, breaking the bubble walls into tiny fragments that cool and solidify quickly.

Pumice and scoria

Chunks of frothy magma that cool and solidify before they land are known as **pumice.** Pieces of pumice are full of air pockets; this makes pumice light enough to float on water. **Scoria** is also full of air pockets but is generally much more dense than pumice. During less violent eruptions, pumice and scoria often land around the vent of a volcano, building up a **cone** of loose material.

Spatter

Spatter is made up of blobs of magma that land before solidifying. It is formed during less violent eruptions of thin, liquid magma. Spatter sometimes pools together to form **lava flows** and sometimes solidifies to build up spatter cones.

Pyroclastic bombs light up the night sky during an eruption of Yasour, a stratovolcano on the Pacific island of Vanuatu.

Lapilli and bombs

Pyroclasts larger than ash, between ¹⁄₁₀ inch (2.5 millimeters) and 2½ inches (63.5 millimeters) in size, are known as **lapilli.** Any larger pyroclast is called a **pyroclastic bomb.** Some bombs solidify before landing. Other bombs stay liquid and spread out when they land. Others are similar to giant, soft-centered candies; these bombs open and release their lava when they land.

STROMBOLI

The volcano on the island of Stromboli, Italy, has erupted nearly continuously since ancient times. It produces ash, spatter, scoria, lapilli, and bombs, which are thrown 300 to 600 feet (90 to 180 meters) above the vent. Some **ejecta** land hundreds of feet away, creating a hazard for visitors to the summit. In 1930, a major eruption on Stromboli threw pyroclastic bombs more than 1 mile (1.6 kilometers), killing six people and destroying several houses.

ASH AND ERUPTION COLUMNS

An eruption column rises from the summit of Popocatépetl, a stratovolcano in Mexico. The column from this 1993 eruption reached an altitude of 1.8 miles (3 kilometers).

Ash is created when bubbly **magma** explodes. The more explosive an eruption is, the more of the magma is turned into ash. Many cubic miles of ash are made by the biggest eruptions. The ash forms clouds that stretch high into Earth's **atmosphere.**

Eruption columns

During an explosive eruption, gas rushes out of a volcano's **vent** at speeds of up to 1,000 miles (1,600 kilometers) per hour. This rush of gas sends ash high into the air. The rapid upward movement of the gas also draws in air from the sides and heats it up. The rising cloud of gases, ash, and hot air is called an **eruption column.** Eruption columns have been known to reach heights of 35 miles (56 kilometers). The gas in the eruption column is lighter than the air

AVIATION HAZARDS

Eruption columns are a hazard to aircraft because ash can clog jet engines. In 1982, a British Airways Boeing 747 flew into an eruption column at 36,000 feet (11,000 meters) over Java in Indonesia. It was night, and the pilots could not see the column. One by one, all four of the jet's engines stopped. The plane lost nearly all its **altitude** before the crew managed to restart the engines and make an emergency landing.

around it, so it floats upward, carrying the ash with it. This process is called **convective rise,** and it can carry ash more than 10 miles (16 kilometers) into the atmosphere.

Ash

High-level winds carry gas and ash in the eruption column away from the volcano. Ash can travel hundreds of miles before it finally settles back to the ground. Settling ash is known as *ashfall,* or airfall. If the ash is still hot when it lands, it sticks together to form a type of rock called **tuff.**

Eruption columns and falling ash often block sunlight, causing almost complete darkness near an erupting volcano. The ash erupted by Mount Pinatubo in 1991 darkened the sky above the island of Luzon, in the Philippines (see pages 20–21). Ash also makes it hard to breathe. If it rains, a layer of ash just 4 inches (10 centimeters) thick can soak up enough water to become heavy enough to collapse a roof. Ash also contaminates water supplies and kills crops and other plant life.

Philippine workers wearing face protection clear ash from the streets, after the eruption of Mount Pinatubo.

MOUNT PINATUBO

Mount Pinatubo is a **stratovolcano** on the island of Luzon in the Philippines. It is the highest of a chain of volcanoes in the region that form part of the Ring of Fire. In 1991, Pinatubo erupted for the first time in more than 600 years. This **eruption** was the second largest of the century.

The eruption

The first signs of volcanic activity at Pinatubo were eruptions of steam in April 1991. Emissions of gas in March and April showed that **magma** was rising. These were followed in April to early June by many small **earthquakes.** The main eruption followed on June 15. It lasted for two days and scientists calculated that it measured 6 on the **Volcanic Explosivity Index.** The eruption blew 850 feet (260 meters) of rock off the volcano, leaving a crater 1¼ miles (2 kilometers) wide. The **eruption column** was 22 miles (35 kilometers) high, and **pyroclastic flows** reached 11 miles (18 kilometers) from the volcano, filling deep valleys with ash deposits up to 660 feet (200 meters) deep.

Pinatubo's effects

Pinatubo's eruption column darkened the region for weeks. Heavy rain mixed with ash lying on the ground and created **lahars.** Ash deposits blocked rivers, which caused flooding. Twenty million

The pyroclastic flows and lahars produced during the 1991 eruption of Mount Pinatubo devastated the surrounding hills.

tons (18 million metric tons) of sulfur dioxide (SO_2) from the eruption spread around the world in three weeks. The gas blocked heat energy from the sun, causing an average global temperature drop of 0.9 °F (0.5 °C).

Human costs

Nearly 200,000 people were evacuated before the eruption, which saved tens of thousands of lives. More than 200,000 were left homeless by the eruption. In all, more than 300 people died as a result of the eruption. A few died in pyroclastic flows and lahars, but most were killed when the roof of the building in which they took shelter collapsed. A **tropical** storm struck soon after the volcano erupted, bringing heavy rains. The rain saturated the layers of ash on roofs, causing them to collapse.

The ash-covered ruins of the village of Dolores, near Mount Pinatubo.

THE AETA

A minority group in the Philippines, the Aeta, made their living on the slopes of the volcano by hunting, gathering, and fishing. The Aeta worshipped Apo Namalyari, the mountain god of Pinatubo, and they considered the volcano to be the center of the universe. The 1991 eruption of Pinatubo displaced the Aeta and so fragmented them that few have returned to their traditional way of life on the volcano.

PYROCLASTIC FLOWS

A **pyroclastic flow** is a cloud made up of hot ash, gas, and, occasionally, larger **pyroclasts.** Pyroclastic flows travel quickly across the ground and are among the most dangerous direct hazards of volcanic **eruptions.**

A pyroclastic flow sweeps down from the Soufrière Hills, a group of volcanic hills on the Caribbean island of Montserrat.

How pyroclastic flows form

Pyroclastic flows form in three different ways. Some form when an **eruption column** becomes too heavy to be supported by **convective rise** and collapses down the sides of a volcano. These flows are made up of gas, ash, and **pumice** and are known as pyroclastic surges. The second type of pyroclastic flow forms when steep-sided **lava domes** on the summit or sides of volcanoes collapse. These flows contain ash and larger

pyroclasts and are known as block and ash flows. The third type forms when one side of a volcano collapses, allowing **magma** to blast out sideways. These flows are known as directed blasts.

How pyroclastic flows move

A pyroclastic flow moves forward because of **gravity.** The larger particles bounce along the ground, and ash swirls above. Block and ash flows often follow valleys, but flows that contain just ash can flow over ridges up to 3,000 feet (900 meters) high. Flows leave behind a layer of ash and other pyroclasts.

Pyroclastic dangers

Pyroclastic flows sweep across the landscape, flattening trees, knocking down buildings, and often killing everything in their path. Victims die from breathing in hot ash and gas, from burns, and from being buried by **debris.** People have survived pyroclastic flows, but only by being hidden from the direct blast and holding their breath until the flow has passed.

EL CHICHÓN

In 1982, El Chichón, a volcano in southern Mexico, unexpectedly erupted. The first eruption, on March 29, produced ash that destroyed houses. The second and third eruptions, a few days later, produced an eruption column that collapsed, forming pyroclastic flows. The flows swept down the volcano's sides, reaching 5 miles (8 kilometers) from the volcano. More than 2,000 people died, and 9 villages were destroyed.

The summit of El Chichón, covered by ash deposits caused by pyroclastic flows.

VESUVIUS

Vesuvius overlooks the Bay of Naples on the west coast of Italy. It is the only **active** volcano on the mainland of Europe. We know that Vesuvius has erupted many times in the past few hundred years, but its most devastating **eruption** was in A.D. 79, when a combination of ashfall and **pyroclastic flows** killed thousands of people.

A street in the ancient Roman city of Pompeii, revealed by digging away pyroclastic deposits from the eruption of Mount Vesuvius. The volcano Vesuvius looms in the background.

The eruption

The eruption began on August 24. An **eruption column** grew, and over the next day 6 feet (2 meters) of hot ash and **pumice** fell around the volcano. Some people in the town of Pompeii died as buildings collapsed under the weight of the ash and pumice. Then, parts of the eruption column collapsed, forming pyroclastic flows. Two flows killed most of the people in the town of Herculaneum, and another swept through Pompeii, killing about 2,000 people who had stayed after the ashfall. In all, more than 3,500 people died. Their bodies were buried in ash, which in some places was 60 feet (18 meters) deep.

The cities were forgotten for more than 1,000 years. In the 1500's, the ruins of Pompeii were discovered by workers digging a water channel. In the 1700's, Herculaneum was discovered during digging for a well. Excavation of the area did not begin until the mid-1700's and remains only partially completed.

THE FIRST EYEWITNESS ACCOUNT

The A.D. 79 eruption of Vesuvius is the first eruption for which we have an eyewitness account. An 18-year-old Roman writer, Gaius Pliny (or Pliny the Younger), watched it from Misenum, a town 18 miles (29 kilometers) away. He described "a great cloud" above the volcano. The cloud spread over Misenum. People panicked, and Pliny fled to the fields with his mother. The next morning, everything was covered with ash. Pliny's uncle, Pliny the Elder, was also a famous writer who was at the time of the eruption commander of the Roman fleet at Pompeii. His ship was trapped on the shore south of the city. He died in a pyroclastic flow, but some of his crew survived. They saw "stones blackened, burned, and broken by the fire" falling on deck and "vast sheets of flame and tongues of fire" from the volcano. Today, explosive eruptions like the one at Vesuvius are known as Plinian eruptions, after Pliny.

Body casts

The objects that have been found in the excavations—an entire ancient Roman city of public and private buildings, forums, streets, an amphitheater, statues and wall paintings, jewelry, pottery, and tools—give us a fascinating view into life some 2,000 years ago. One of the most interesting aspects of the excavations is casts of the victims in the throes of death. Many of the dead at Pompeii were surrounded by a liquid formed of ashes and rain. Eventually, this liquid dried and hardened around the bodies. The bodies turned to dust, leaving a cavity shaped like the body in the hardened ash. In the mid-1800's, excavators began pouring plaster into these cavities. From these human casts, we can see detailed reliefs of the victims of Vesuvius in their last moments.

The cast of a person killed in Pompeii. About 2,000 of the town's inhabitants were killed instantly by pyroclastic flows.

MOUNT PELÉE

Mount Pelée is a **stratovolcano** on the island of Martinique in the French West Indies. In 1902, **pyroclastic flows** from Mount Pelée destroyed the island's city, Saint Pierre, killing about 28,000 people. It was the worst volcanic disaster of the 1900's.

The eruption

Mount Pelée began to erupt on April 24 with a series of small explosions. In February 1902, the inhabitants of Saint Pierre—a colonial city known at that time as the "Paris of the West Indies"—smelled sulfurous gas and felt minor **earthquakes.** In coming days, people grew more alarmed as the intensity of volcanic activity increased. The increased activity caused other strange events to occur. Large numbers of insects and snakes came down into Saint Pierre. Ashfall from the volcano apparently caused these animals to leave areas higher on the mountain. Some 50 people were killed by snakebite in the days preceding the **eruption.**

Visitors walk through the ruined streets of Saint Pierre after the eruption of Mount Pelée in 1902.

On May 5, part of the rim of the summit **crater** collapsed, releasing hot water from the lake in the crater. The water mixed with ash to form a **lahar** that killed 25 people. On May 6, new **magma** reached the surface, creating a **lava dome** in the crater, as well as an **eruption column.** On May 8, just before 8 a.m., the lava dome collapsed, forming a pyroclastic flow. The flow reached Saint Pierre, 4 miles (6 kilometers) away, in less than a minute, flattening the buildings and killing all but a few of the inhabitants who had not fled the island. Villages around Saint Pierre were also destroyed, along with ships in the harbor. One sailor who survived described the pyroclastic flow as a hurricane of fire. The city burned for several days, and on May 20, another flow destroyed anything that was left.

At the time, pyroclastic flows were poorly understood. Saint Pierre had not been evacuated, in part because people thought the danger would come from **lava flows,** which could not reach Saint Pierre. The day before Saint Pierre was hit, thousands of villagers went to the city where they believed they would be safer.

After the disaster, some parts of the city were rebuilt. Today, there is an observatory on the volcano to monitor activity and warn of future eruptions.

Ludger Sylbaris displays scars from the burns he received during the eruption.

THE "ONLY" SURVIVOR

One of the few people in the city of Saint Pierre to survive the pyroclastic flow was a 27-year-old laborer named Ludger Sylbaris (also known as Louis-Auguste Cyparis). He escaped death while in the prison's underground dungeon. His cell had no windows, only a small grate cut above the door. Afterward, Sylbaris described how it suddenly became dark, and hot air and gas came in through the dungeon's air vent. The heat burned his legs, arms, and back, but he held his breath so his lungs were unharmed. He was rescued four days after the eruption. Eventually, Sylbaris joined the Barnum and Bailey circus, where he was billed, with much exaggeration, as "the only living object that survived in the silent city of death."

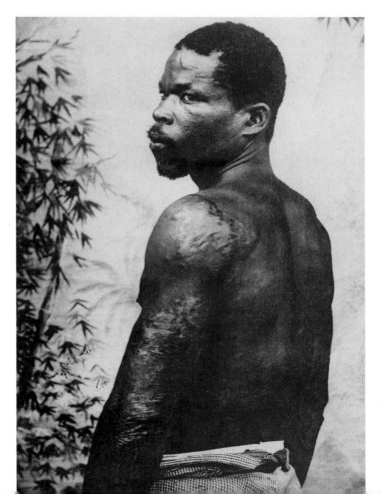

LAHARS, LANDSLIDES, AND FLOODS

Mud deposited by lahars during the 1991 eruption covers the slopes of Mount Pinatubo in the Philippines.

Lahars, landslides, and floods are some of the main secondary hazards of an **eruption.** A volcanic lahar—a mixture of water and volcanic ash that flows down the sides of a volcano or along river valleys—is sometimes called a mudflow. Only **pyroclastic flows** are more dangerous than lahars. Eruptions can also set off landslides of volcanic **debris,** or debris avalanches, and **tsunamis.**

How lahars move

The water in lahars can come from **crater** lakes found at the tops of volcanoes, from snow and ice melted by pyroclastic flows, from thunderstorms that form inside **eruption columns,** and from any rain that falls after an eruption. Lahars can move at speeds of up to 90 miles (145 kilometers) per hour and can travel more than 100 miles (160 kilometers) from a volcano before stopping.

The effects of lahars

The mixture of water and ash in lahars is very thick and dense, like unset concrete. Fast-moving lahars carry along trees, boulders, and other debris. Lahars naturally flow down valleys, often destroying towns or villages that lie in their path. When a lahar reaches flat ground, it slows down and spreads out, covering everything with a thick, semisolid layer of mud and debris. The muddy deposits sometimes block river channels, causing floods upstream.

In 1996, an icecap flood left this wide plain of mud in southern Iceland. The flood damaged the bridge in the foreground.

Tsunamis

Explosive eruptions, landslides that fall into the sea, and pyroclastic flows can cause giant waves called tsunamis. A tsunami wave can travel across open water at hundreds of miles per hour. In the middle of seas and oceans, the wave may be only a few feet high and hardly noticeable. But as it reaches the shallow water near a coast, it slows down and becomes much higher. When a tsunami wave washes ashore, it can cause widespread destruction and flooding. In 1792, a landslide that followed an eruption of Japan's Mount Unzen created a tsunami that killed nearly 15,000 people in Shimbara City and nearby areas.

ICECAP FLOODS

Thick sheets of ice, called icecaps, cover some volcanoes. During an eruption, the intense heat melts the ice closest to the cone, causing a body of water to be trapped under the outer ice. Eventually, the water breaks through the ice, causing a sudden flood. These floods are common in Iceland, where they are known as *jökulhlaups,* which means *glacier bursts.*

THE ARMERO LAHAR

The ruins of Armero, Colombia, after a giant lahar flowed through the town.

On Nov. 13, 1985, the Nevado del Ruiz volcano in Colombia erupted. A subsequent **lahar** buried the town of Armero, killing more than 23,000 people and injuring 5,000 others.

The eruption

Nevado del Ruiz is a **stratovolcano.** With a height of 17,717 feet (5,400 meters), the volcano's summit is always covered with snow and ice. The 1985 **eruption** was not very violent, but **pyroclastic**

flows melted ice and snow, releasing millions of tons of water. The water mixed with ash and other rocky material to form lahars that rushed down narrow valleys on the sides of the volcano. The lahars traveled more than 60 miles (100 kilometers) from the volcano.

The town of Armero

The town of Armero was about 46 miles (74 kilometers) from Nevado del Ruiz and lay at the end of a steep-sided valley. After the eruption of the Nevado del Ruiz volcano, a series of lahars poured down the valley and spread out over the town. One wave of mud was 130 feet (40 meters) high. The flow swept away buildings, trees, people, and animals. It struck at night, when most people were in bed and had little chance of escape. Three out of four townspeople were buried alive.

A survivor's account

A taxi driver, Modesto Bocanegra Menesses, survived the destruction of Armero. He was asleep when the lahar hit. The force of the flow knocked down his house and carried him about 2 miles (3 kilometers) away. He was hit again and again by debris. "The mud grabbed me and pushed me under. I would come up again and again. I couldn't breathe," he said later. Bocanegra lost his wife, two of his three daughters, and most other members of his family in the lahar.

WARNINGS IGNORED

Armero was built on old lahars that had killed people hundreds of years ago. Local **volcanologists** warned that an eruption was on the way and lahars were likely, but there was no emergency plan. The authorities did not order an evacuation until it was too late. Instead, they told people to stay in their homes. Armero has not been rebuilt—its ruins are buried under the hardened mud.

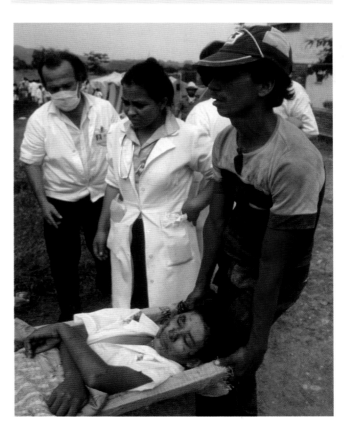

A survivor is carried away by rescue workers. Many survivors were pulled from the mud by helicopters.

The **eruption** of Mount Pinatubo in 1991 (see pages 20-21) was the second largest of the last 100 years, but it was minor compared with giant volcanic eruptions that have occurred in the past. Giant eruptions can spread ash for thousands of miles and affect the weather globally.

The spread of sulfur dioxide into the atmosphere soon after the eruption of Mount Pinatubo (top) and two months later (bottom). In the atmosphere, the sulfur dioxide mixes with water to form particles that block sunlight. These particles, combined with volcanic ash, cool temperatures on Earth. After Pinatubo erupted, average global temperatures dropped by about 0.9 °F (0.5°C). The eruption of the supervolcano Toba lowered average global temperature as much as 9 °F (5 °C.)

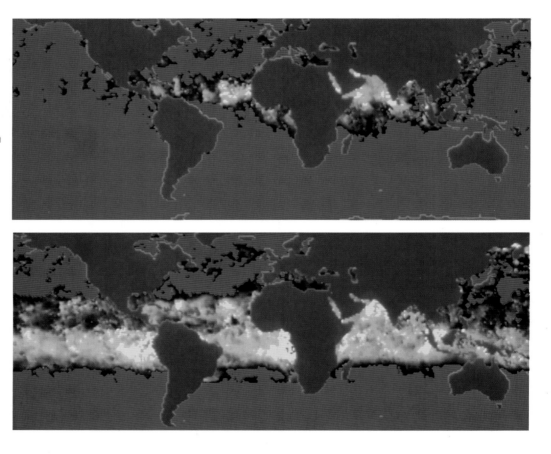

Giant calderas

A **caldera** *(kal DIHR uh)* is a huge depression in Earth's surface formed when the ground collapses into a hole left behind by erupting **magma.** The largest calderas, sometimes called **supervolcanoes**—form where vast pools of magma collect below the surface. Because magma in these volcanoes is very **viscous** and traps a lot of gases, supervolcanoes erupt a huge amount of magma that has been under tremendous pressure. Then, it may take hundreds of thousands of years for such a volcano to erupt again. As the large amount of material erupts, the overlying rock collapses, forming a huge depression.

The Toba eruption

The island of Sumatra in Indonesia had a caldera volcano, named Toba, which erupted about 74,000 years ago. The eruption produced 300 times as much ash as the 1991 eruption of Mount Pinatubo and left a caldera 60 miles (97 kilometers) long and 18 miles (29 kilometers) wide. Ash piled to a depth of 4 inches (10 centimeters) at a distance of 1,900 miles (3,100 kilometers) from the eruption. **Volcanologists** calculate that the eruption measured 8 on the **Volcanic Explosivity Index.** Toba caused an average fall in global temperature of between 5 and 9 °F (3 and 5 °C). This fall in temperature may have killed as many as half the trees in the Northern Hemisphere.

YELLOWSTONE

There has not been an eruption of a supervolcano in modern times, and the sites of many from the past remain undetected. Perhaps the most well-known and most-visited supervolcano is in Yellowstone National Park in the western United States. The caldera of the Yellowstone supervolcano is about 45 miles (70 kilometers) by 30 miles (50 kilometers), and forms a major portion of the park.

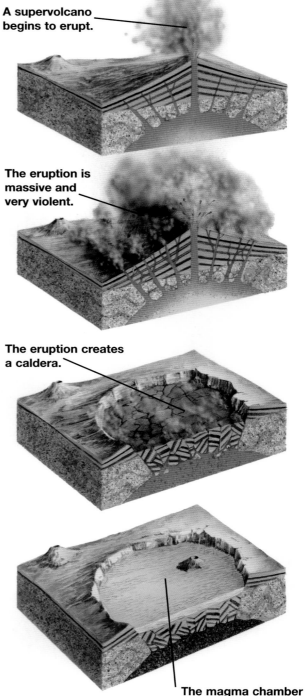

THE FORMATION OF A CALDERA BY THE ERUPTION OF A SUPERVOLCANO

A supervolcano begins to erupt.

The eruption is massive and very violent.

The eruption creates a caldera.

The magma chamber beneath the caldera solidifies and the volcano becomes dormant or extinct. The caldera may then fill with water to form a lake.

YELLOWSTONE VOLCANO OBSERVATORY

Yellowstone National Park is a popular tourist destination, partially because of its volcanic activity. There are hundreds of **geysers** and thousands of hot springs and bubbling mud pools. The park sits over one of the world's largest **caldera** complexes. **Volcanologists** at the Yellowstone Volcano Observatory monitor the caldera carefully because it is **active** and so may erupt again in the future.

Eruptions at Yellowstone

The Yellowstone caldera is over a **hot spot** in Earth's **crust.** The caldera formed about 640,000 years ago when the ground collapsed into a **magma chamber** after a gigantic **eruption,** which has been ranked as an 8 on the **Volcanic Explosivity Index.** The eruption produced 500 times as much material as the eruption of Mount Saint Helens in 1981. **Pyroclastic flows** left layers of **tuff** up to 1,300 feet (400 meters) thick, and ash from the eruption has been found nearly everywhere in what is now the United States. Two other large calderas close by were formed by eruptions about 1.3 million years ago and 2.1 million years ago.

The Yellowstone caldera, created by an eruption 640,000 years ago, underlies much of Yellowstone National Park.

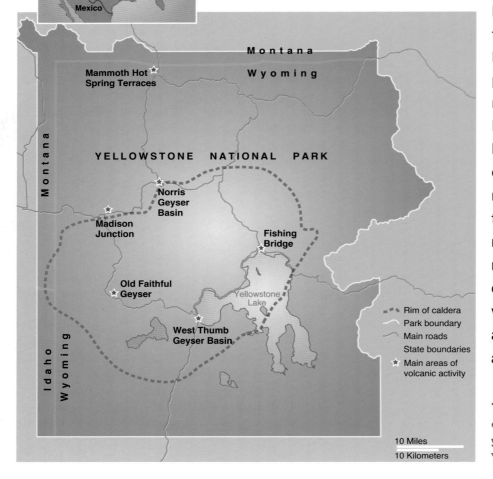

The Observatory

The Yellowstone Volcano Observatory (YVO) was erected in 2001 to monitor volcanic activity in the Yellowstone caldera. The U.S. Geological Survey (USGS), Yellowstone National Park, and the University of Utah operate it jointly. The YVO incorporates a network of **seismometers** to monitor earthquakes and a network of **global positioning system** (GPS) stations to monitor ground movements. Data are sent from the networks to the University of Utah to be recorded and analyzed. Dozens of small earthquakes are detected every month, as the center of the caldera rises by about 2.5 inches (6.4 centimeters) a year, but there are no signs that another eruption will occur anytime soon. A survey using seismometers has shown a magma chamber underneath the caldera measuring 37 miles (60 kilometers) by 25 miles (40 kilometers) and 10 miles (16 kilometers) deep.

Geysers—and other places where superheated water rises to the surface—are evidence of the immense volcanic activity beneath Yellowstone's scenic terrain.

A CATASTROPHIC ERUPTION

Another event similar to the eruption 640,000 years ago would be catastrophic for North America and the world. Its effects are difficult to imagine. The amount of ash in the sky from such an event would cause the temperature of Earth to become much colder. Half of the United States could be covered in ash up to 3 feet (1 meter) deep. The disruption to agriculture in the U.S. could lead to famine and starvation globally. Human civilization would be challenged to survive. Fortunately, scientists do not think Yellowstone shows any signs of an eruption on this scale within the next few centuries.

KRAKATAU

Krakatau is one of a line of volcanoes between the islands of Sumatra and Java in Indonesia. Parts of the volcano's top form the islands of Krakatau, Anak Krakatau, Sertung (Lang), and Payang (Verlaten).

The eruption

Before the **eruption,** Krakatau was a huge **stratovolcano** standing 2,667 feet (813 meters) above sea level. The eruption began in May 1883, but the main eruption came on August 27. Scientists calculate that the eruption measured 6 on the **Volcanic Explosivity Index.** A series of gigantic explosions on the morning of August 27 created an **eruption column** that was probably more than 15 miles (24 kilometers) high and huge **pyroclastic flows.** The final blast blew the island apart and was heard 3,000 miles (4,800 kilometers) away. Then, two-thirds of the island collapsed into the empty **magma chamber,** creating a **caldera** 4 miles (6 kilometers) below sea level.

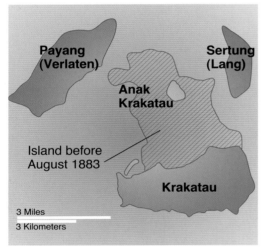

Payang
(Verlaten)

Sertung
(Lang)

Anak
Krakatau

Island before
August 1883

Krakatau

3 Miles
3 Kilometers

The 1883 eruption of Krakatau destroyed much of the island (shaded blue). Anak Krakatau is a new island forming in the caldera of the volcano. Payang (Verlaten) and Sertung (Lang) islands are remnants of older volcanic islands.

Krakatau lies in the Sunda Strait of Indonesia, between the islands of Sumatra and Java.

Philippines

M a l a y s i a

I N D O N E S I A

Sumatra

Lampong Bay

Sunda Strait

Krakatau

Sebuku
Sebesi

J a v a

S e a

Java

Indian

Ocean

East
Timor

Australia

500 Miles
500 Kilometers

Krakatau's effects

The pyroclastic flows killed several thousand people on nearby islands. The combination of the pyroclastic flows and the collapse of the volcano into the sea also caused a series of **tsunamis** up to 130 feet (40 meters) high that killed 36,000 people on the coasts of Sumatra and Java. People living up to 500 miles (800 kilometers) away were killed, and some islands close to Krakatau were completely submerged. Ash blown into the **atmosphere** caused spectacular red sunsets around the world for the next three years. Scientists estimate that 30 million tons (27 million metric tons) of sulfur dioxide (SO_2) were released, which caused world temperatures to fall by up to 0.9 °F (0.5 °C) for the next five years.

Krakatau erupting in an 1888 illustration.

FALL OF ATLANTIS?

A volcanic eruption often compared with Krakatau's occurred at Thera (now called Santorini), an island in the Mediterranean Sea, near Crete. Scientists have recently determined, however, that the 1650 B.C. eruption at Santorini was actually twice as large as previously thought. New data shows that the volcano at Santorini ejected 14 cubic miles (58 cubic kilometers) of hot ash and **lava.** That is six times the amount of **ejecta** erupted from Krakatau. The eruption at Santorini is thought to have led to the fall of the ancient Minoan civilization. Additionally, some scientists think that the legend of the lost continent of Atlantis might not be a legend. According to some experts, the description of Atlantis, the place said to have sank beneath the waves "in a single day and night of misfortune," matches the island of Thera.

MOUNT TAMBORA

Mount Tambora, on the island of Sumbawa in Indonesia, lies in the same line of **stratovolcanoes** as Krakatau. Tambora lies along the Ring of Fire, over a **subduction zone** where the Indian-Australian **tectonic plate** moves beneath the Eurasian tectonic plate. The volcano last erupted in 1815. Scientists calculate that the **eruption** measured 7 on the **Volcanic Explosivity Index.** It was probably one of the largest eruptions in the last 10,000 years, and it had serious long-term effects on the world's weather.

The caldera of Mount Tambora appears as a dark disk in a photograph of the island of Sumbawa taken aboard the U.S. space shuttle.

The eruption

The eruption of Mount Tambora began on April 5, 1815, when an explosion created an **eruption column** 21 miles (34 kilometers) high. The eruption became more violent on April 15, when a new column 27 miles (43 kilometers) high formed. Hundreds of thousands of tons of ash poured into the air every second. In all, the eruption produced 12 cubic miles (50 cubic kilometers) of ash and about 80 million tons (72 million metric tons) of sulfur dioxide (SO_2). **Pyroclastic flows** covered the island. The eruption destroyed Tambora's summit, leaving a **caldera** 4 miles (6.4 kilometers) across.

Effects

Just 26 of Sumbawa's 10,000 inhabitants survived the pyroclastic flows. People on the islands of Bali and Lombok, 100 miles (160 kilometers) away, died when their homes collapsed under the weight of ash. The ashfall also killed crops, causing a famine that resulted in the deaths of thousands of others. Altogether, an estimated 60,000 people died because of the eruption.

Ash and gas from the **eruption column** spread around the world, reducing the amount of heat reaching Earth's surface. The average global temperature fell by about 0.9 °F (0.5 °C). However, in parts of Europe and eastern North America, the temperature fell by more than 3.0 °F (1.7 °C), and in North America, 1816 became known as "the year without a summer." New England experienced snow and frosts during the summer months, resulting in the loss of nearly all crops.

CROP FAILURES

In 1816, the crops failed because of the cold and lack of sunlight. Shortages of food led to famines and epidemics of disease in Europe and India. There were riots in France because the price of grain was so high. Many people left their homes and traveled thousands of miles to search for better living conditions.

This 1816 ilustration shows Brooklyn, New York, during the severe winter weather caused by the eruption of Mount Tambora.

RESCUE AND AID

Millions of people live in places where they are at risk from such volcanic hazards as ashfall, **pyroclastic flows,** and **lahars.** In many of these areas, there are official emergency plans ready to be used during an **eruption.** The authorities take advice from **volcanologists** to decide whether to evacuate people. Maps of the places around a volcano that are most at risk (called hazard maps) help volcanologists to make their decisions.

The town of Salem on the island of Montserrat was evacuated in 1997 because of ash from the eruption of the Soufrière Hills volcano.

Rescue

It is not always possible to warn people in remote areas about eruptions, and sometimes people do not want to leave their homes. Then the priority is to rescue those who have been injured or are trapped and also to evacuate survivors in case of further eruptions.

These rescues occur on a massive scale, involving all branches of the emergency services and often military forces as well. Rescue efforts are often very difficult—roads blocked by ashfall or lahars restrict rescuers' access and damaged communication systems hinder the coordination of emergency services. Further, ash in the air can prevent aircraft from functioning.

Shelter and aid

People who have been evacuated need temporary shelter, food, and water. Where homes have been destroyed, evacuees need long-term help. Deep ash deposits and the threat of further eruptions often mean that towns and villages have to be abandoned for good. Some of the most destructive volcanoes are in less developed countries of the world, where governments cannot cope with large-scale disasters. Farmers who lose their homes, crops, and livestock are left with nothing. In these cases, international aid is required to set up camps, to supply water and food, and to help rebuild homes and infrastructure.

A mechanical loader is used to build a dam to stop lava from reaching a town on the slopes of Mount Etna, Italy.

VOLCANO DEFENSES

In a few places, people have built defenses against volcanic eruptions. Special dams called **sabo dams** are common in Japan and Indonesia. These dams allow lahars that occur—especially after rainfall—to flow normally, but they block the debris carried by the lahar. **Lava flows** have also been diverted by building barriers. Often, earthen barriers are erected to divert lava flows when their path threatens towns or structures.

FIGHTING AGAINST VOLCANOES—HEIMAEY

The island of Heimaey lies 8 miles (13 kilometers) off the south coast of Iceland. The town of Vestmannaeyjar, with a population of about 4,500, was built around the island's natural harbor and is a busy fishing port. In 1973, **lava flows** from an **eruption** threatened to block the harbor. The people of Vestmannaeyjar fought to stop the flow and save their livelihoods.

The eruption

On January 23, the ground split open near Vestmannaeyjar, and **lava,** ash, **scoria,** and steam began to pour out. The ground continued to open up, eventually forming a fissure (or crack) nearly 1 mile (1.6 kilometers) long. After a few days, the fissure became blocked with cooling lava, but lava continued to flow out of one main **vent.** The eruption finally stopped in early July, nearly five months later.

A curtain of lava spews from a fissure (crack) on the Icelandic island of Heimaey in 1973, threatening houses in the town of Vestmannaeyjar.

Effects of the eruption

Ash and scoria from the eruption fell on Vestmannaeyjar. Scoria and **spatter** formed a new **cone** 600 feet (180 meters) high on the outskirts of the town. Lava flows spread into the town and down to the sea near the harbor. About a third of Vestmannaeyjar was destroyed by lava flows, but no one was killed by the eruption itself.

Fighting the lava

Nearly all the people of Heimaey were evacuated when the eruption began. A team of volunteers tried to save homes by removing ash and scoria from roofs. They also tried to stop the lava flows from reaching the harbor by cooling them. They set up 43 pumps and 19 miles (30 kilometers) of pipes to carry seawater to the flows. In all, they sprayed 6 million tons (5 million metric tons) of water onto the lava. Some flows partly blocked the harbor entrance, but others were stopped, and the harbor was saved.

Cooled magma that erupted from a fissure on Heimaey added to the island along its northeastern coast.

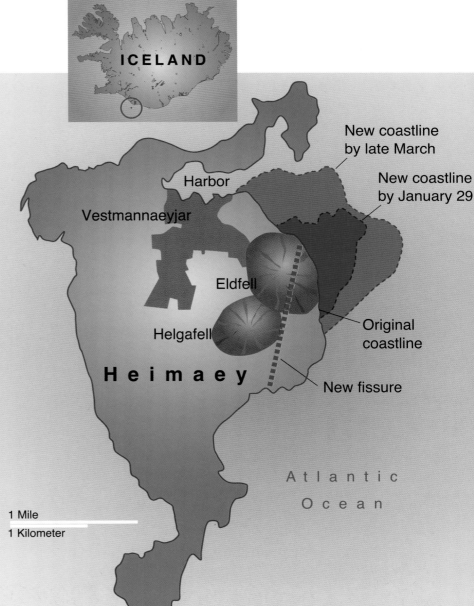

VOLCANISM IN ICELAND

Iceland stands on top of the Mid-Atlantic Ridge, which is a **divergent boundary** between two **tectonic plates.** The ridge is 12,500 miles (20,000 kilometers) long, and **magma** pushing up from the ridge forms hundreds of undersea volcanoes. Iceland has been built up by eruptions over tens of millions of years. Heimaey was formed by an eruption about 5,000 years ago.

ICELAND

New coastline by late March

New coastline by January 29

Harbor

Vestmannaeyjar

Eldfell

Helgafell

H e i m a e y

Original coastline

New fissure

A t l a n t i c   O c e a n

1 Mile

1 Kilometer

A CINDER CONE

You will need

- A flexible drinking straw
- A sheet of cardboard about 12 inches (30 centimeters) by 8 inches (20 centimeters)
- A sharp pencil
- A large tray
- Granulated sugar
- Adhesive tape

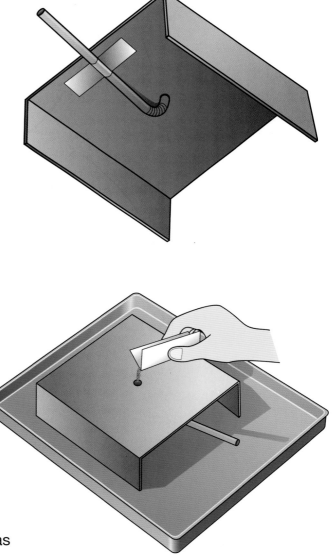

1. Using the pencil, make a hole in the center of the cardboard. Fold down about 2 inches (5 centimeters) of cardboard at each end to make supports.

2. Push the short end of the straw into the hole from underneath so that the tip of the straw is level with the top surface of the cardboard. Tape the straw in place underneath the cardboard.

3. Stand the cardboard on the tray with the straw bent so that you can blow into it.

4. Make a crease in a scrap of paper and pour a little sugar onto it. Pour the sugar down the end of the straw in the cardboard.

5. Now very carefully blow into the bottom end of the straw. Don't blow too hard.

The sugar will be blown out of the straw and will build up a cone around the tip of the straw, just as scoria builds up a cone around a volcano's vent.

active A term applied to volcanoes that have erupted in the last 10,000 years.

altitude A measure of height above Earth's surface or sea level.

asthenosphere A part of Earth's mantle formed of a layer of hot, soft rock.

atmosphere The layer of gases surrounding Earth.

caldera A huge crater or dip in the landscape formed when the ground collapses into a hole left by erupting magma.

conduit The central tube through which magma emerges from a volcano.

cone A heap of volcanic ash and lava that forms around a vent during a volcanic eruption.

convective rise When hot volcanic gases and air rise up into the atmosphere because of their low density, forming an eruption column.

convergent plate boundary A boundary between two tectonic plates where the plates are moving toward each other.

core The center part of Earth's interior, lying below the mantle.

crater A bowl-shaped hollow in the ground caused by an explosion, an impact, or an underground collapse.

crust The solid outer layer of Earth.

debris Rubble, broken objects, and other damaged material.

divergent plate boundary A boundary between two tectonic plates wherein the plates are moving away from each other. Divergent plate boundaries are mostly on ocean floors.

dormant An active volcano that is not erupting or about to erupt.

earthquake A shaking of the ground caused by the sudden movement of underground rock.

ejecta Matter ejected, as from a volcano.

eruption The pouring out of gases, ash, lava, and rocks from a volcano.

eruption column (also called an **eruption cloud**) A tall cloud of gas and ash that has erupted from a volcano.

extinct A volcano that is unlikely to erupt again.

geyser A spring that throws up hot water with explosive force from time to time. Often, the water shoots up in great columns, cloudy with steam.

global positioning system (GPS) A navigation system in which a receiver calculates its position by detecting signals from satellites.

gravity The effect of the force of attraction that acts between objects because of their mass — that is, the amount of matter the objects have.

hot spot An underground concentration of heat that creates volcanoes.

lahar (also called a **mudflow**) A volcanic mudflow, made up of water and ash.

landslide A mass of soil and rock that slides down a slope.

lapilli Pyroclasts between $\frac{1}{10}$ inch (2.5 millimeters) and 2.5 inches (63.5 millimeters) in size.

lava Molten rock that flows out of a volcano.

lava dome A steep-sided mound formed by the eruption of thick, viscous lava.

lava flow An outpouring of lava that flows over the surface of land.

lava fountain A vertical eruption of lava.

lithosphere A layer of Earth, made up of the crust and the upper region of the mantle, which forms the tectonic plates of Earth. The lithosphere is solid and rests on top of the asthenosphere.

magma Molten rock beneath Earth's surface.

magma chamber A cavity under a volcano filled with magma.

mantle The layer of rock between Earth's crust and core.

molten Melted by heat.

pumice Pieces of solidified, frothy magma that are full of air spaces, making them very light.

pyroclast A fragment of magma tossed into the air by expanding gas.

pyroclastic bomb A fragment of magmatic rock that is blown out during an eruption; pyroclastic bombs can range in size from 2½ inches (63.5 millimeters) to many feet (meters) in diameter.

pyroclastic flow A cloud of hot ash and gas that travels at great speed, mostly along the ground.

radar An electronic device for determining the distance, direction, and speed of objects by the reflection of radio waves.

sabo dam A dam designed to allow lahars to flow normally but to block the debris carried by a lahar.

satellite An object that continuously orbits Earth or some other body in space. People use artificial satellites for such tasks as collecting data.

scoria (also called **cinders**) Pieces of solidified magma that are full of air spaces.

seismology The study of earthquakes and other movements of Earth's crust.

seismometer An instrument for recording the direction, intensity, and duration of earthquakes or other movements of Earth's crust.

side vent An opening on the slope of a volcano, where ash, gas, and lava come out onto the surface.

spatter Blobs of magma that land before solidifying.

stratovolcano (also called a **composite cone**) A cone-shaped volcano made up of successive layers of ash and lava.

subduction When the edge of one of the tectonic plates that make up Earth's surface sinks below a neighboring plate.

subduction zone A region where one tectonic plate slides under another at a convergent plate boundary.

supervolcano A volcano that forms a huge, underground pool of thick magma. Such volcanoes then erupt, ejecting huge amounts of magma. A caldera (depression) remains when the eruption is finished. It may take hundreds of thousands of years for a volcano of this nature to erupt again.

tectonic plate One of about 30 rigid pieces making up Earth's surface.

tiltmeter An instrument that measures upward and downward movements of the ground.

tropical To do with the tropics, the regions of Earth that lie about 1,600 miles (2,570 kilometers) north or south of the equator.

tsunami A series of powerful ocean waves produced by an earthquake, landslide, volcanic eruption, or asteroid impact.

tuff A type of rock formed from layers of volcanic ash.

vent The hole in a volcano where ash, gas, and lava come out onto the surface.

viscosity A measure of the resistance of a fluid to flow.

viscous Something that is thick and sticky.

Volcanic Explosivity Index (VEI) A scale used to rate the power of an eruption. An eruption with a VEI of 0 is not explosive at all, while one with a VEI of 8 ranks among the most explosive eruptions known.

volcanic neck (also called a **volcanic plug**) A rock formation made up of the solidified magma from the center of an ancient volcano. The solid magma remains upright after erosion has stripped away the surrounding material.

volcanologist A scientist who studies volcanoes.

water vapor Water in the form of a gas.

BOOKS

Eyewitness Books, Volcanoes and Earthquakes, by James Putnam and Susanna Van Rose, Dorling Kindersley, 2004.

Into the Volcano: A Volcano Researcher at Work, by Donna O' Meara, Kids Can Press, 2005.

Volcanoes, by Judith and Dennis Fradin, National Geographic Children's Books, 2007.

Volcanoes, by Trudi Strain Trueit, Franklin Watts, 2003.

Volcanoes in Human History: The Far-Reaching Effects of Major Eruptions, by Jelle Zeilinga de Boer and Donald Theodore Sanders, Princeton, 2004.

Will It Blow? Become a Volcano Detective at Mount St. Helens, by Elizabeth Rusch, Sasquatch Books, 2007.

WEB SITES

http://science.howstuffworks.com/volcano.htm

http://volcano.und.edu/

http://volcanoes.usgs.gov/

http://www.cotf.edu/ete/modules/volcanoes/vmtvesuvius.html

http://www.volcanoes.com/

INDEX

EAU CLAIRE DISTRICT LIBRARY